STRIPED EARRINGS

You need:

Two 2 inch (5 cm) paper squares

Two 1³⁄₄ inch (4 cm) paper squares

Two 1¹⁄₂ inch (3 cm) paper squares

Glue

Earring fittings

---

1. Follow the directions for the simple earrings. Align the papers into two equal stacks with the smallest units on top. Slide the top corners into each other.

2. Glue together at the back. Attach earring fittings.

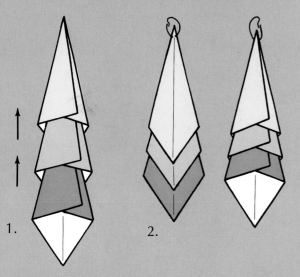

1.

2.

PIN OR HAIR ORNAMENT

Fold one striped earring and glue it to a pin back, hair barrette or comb.

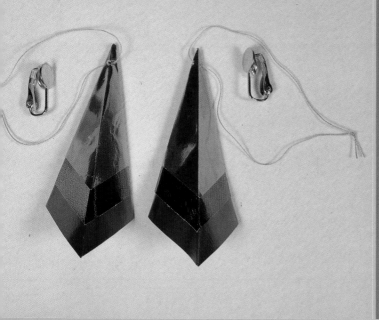

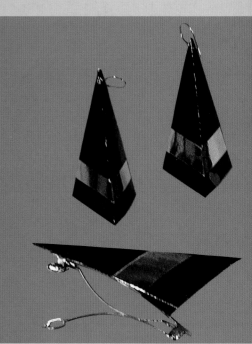

WHALE PENDANT, NECKLACE AND EARRINGS

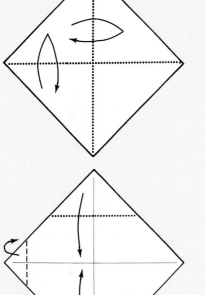

1.

2.

3.

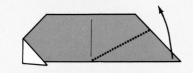

4.

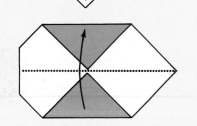

5.

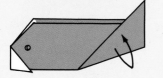

6.

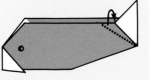

7.

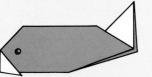

WHALE PENDANT

You need:

One 3 inch (7 cm) paper square

---

1. With white side of paper up, fold the square on the diagonal. Unfold. Fold on the other diagonal. Unfold.

2a. Fold the top and bottom corners to the center.

2b. Fold the left corner to the *back*.

3. Fold the paper in half.

4. Fold the tail up.

5. Fold the tail down again. Then tuck it in between the main layers of paper on the creases made in step 4.

6. Fold the back corner to the inside, first on the front, then on the back.

Optional: Glue the top edges together. Stuff small pieces of tissue into the body. This makes the whale three-dimensional.

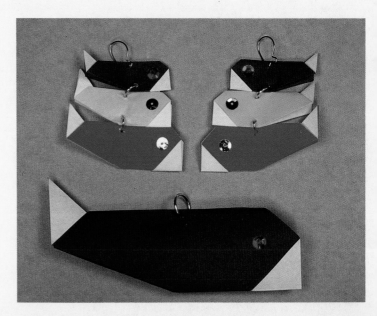

NECKLACE

Make three or more whales. Attach them to a ribbon or beaded necklace with loops of yarn, small pieces of wire or jump rings (sold in craft and bead stores).

EARRINGS

You can make earrings with single whales from 2 inch (5 cm) paper squares. The earrings with three whales are made from $1\frac{1}{2}$, $1\frac{3}{4}$ and 2 inch squares (3, 4 and 5 cm).

MALTESE CROSS

NECKLACE

You need:

One 4 inch (10 cm) paper square—different colors on front and back are best

1 yard (1 m) satin cord or ribbon

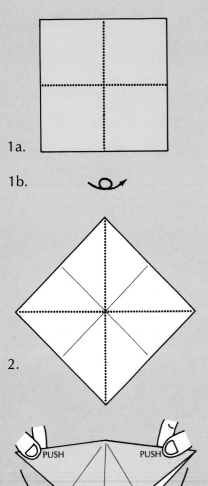

1a.

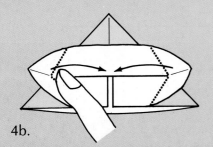

1b.

1a. Fold the square on the dotted lines shown.

1b. Turn paper over.

2. Fold on the diagonal. Unfold. Fold on the other diagonal. Do not unfold.

3. Hold the paper on the last crease exactly as shown. Push paper toward the middle into a triangle. Make sure triangle has two flaps on each side. If you have three flaps on one side, flip one over.

4a. Bring the bottom edge of the front layer of paper up to about two-thirds of the height of the triangle.

4b. Make a sharp crease by sliding your forefinger from one end to the other. Corners will stand up. Bring the corners to the middle and squash them flat. See next drawing.

5. Turn paper over and repeat steps 4a and 4b on the back.

6. Flip the right flap over to the left, like turning the page of a book. Turn paper over and repeat on the back, again flipping from right to left.

7. Fold the front layer up as far as it will go. Repeat on the back.

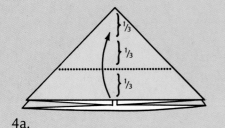

4a.

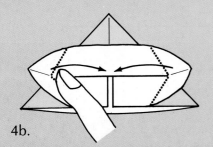

4b.

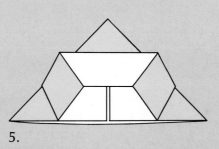

5.

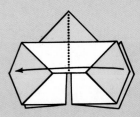

6.

8. Arrange the four "arms" into a cross shape. Pinching at the center helps. Find the two "pockets" at the end of each arm. Poke into each pocket with your forefinger or a pencil and squash the top of each pocket.

9. Pierce a hole at the end of one arm of the cross. Thread the cord through the hole. Balance the cross at the middle of the cord. Tie a knot about 1 inch (2 cm) away. Wear the necklace by tying the cord at the back of the neck.

EARRINGS

You need:

Two $2\frac{1}{2}$ inch (6 cm) paper squares—different colors on front and back are best

Earring fittings

___

Follow steps 1 through 8 for the necklace. Attach earring fittings.

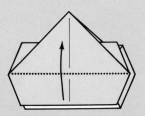

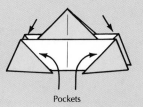

7.

8.

Pockets

JEWELRY BOX

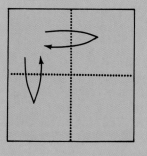

1.

 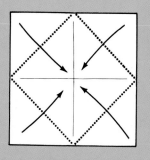

2.

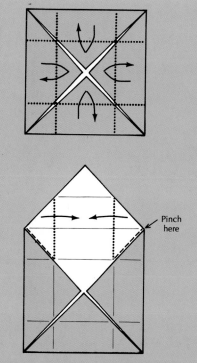

3.

4.

5.

JEWELRY BOX

You need:

One 10 inch (25 cm) paper square

___

1. If paper is colored on one side only, begin with colored side up. Fold paper in half both ways. Unfold.

2. *Turn paper over.*

3. Fold the four corners to the middle.

4. Fold the four *edges* to the middle. Unfold each time.

5. Lift up one flap. Pinch the right corner and push it over to the left. Now pinch the left corner and push it over to the right.

6. Bring down the flap, locking in both corners. The sides of the box form. Lift up the flap on the opposite side of the box and lock in the other two corners. Sharpen all edges.

Pinch here

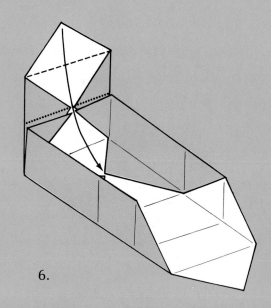

6.

BOX COVER:
You can make a cover to fit over the box. In step 3 do not fold all the way to the middle, but leave a space of about $\frac{1}{4}$ inch (5 mm).

GIFT BOXES:
You can make boxes of any size by using smaller or larger squares. You can also make shallower boxes. In step 4 do not fold the four edges all the way to the middle.

JEWELRY CHEST:
Make a box with a cover from 20 inch (50 cm) squares of heavy paper.

SPACE RING

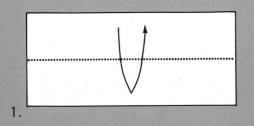

1.

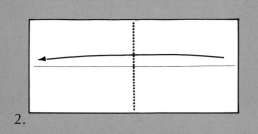

2.

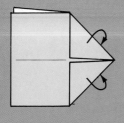

3.

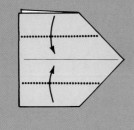

4.

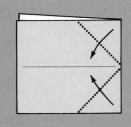

5.

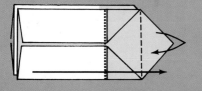

6.

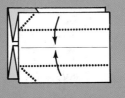

7.

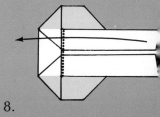

8.

SPACE RING

You can fold this ring from an ordinary piece of paper, but it is a real show-stopper when you make it from a dollar bill. It's not difficult but requires a lot of folding.

You need:

A dollar bill or paper 6 inches by $2\frac{1}{2}$ inches (15 cm by 7 cm)

1. With green side up, fold bill in half lengthwise. Unfold.

2. Fold in half the short way.

3. Bring the corners at the folded edge to the middle crease.

4. Unfold the corners and tuck them in between the main layers of the paper, on the creases just made.

5. On the front, fold the top and bottom edges to the middle. Turn the paper over and repeat on the back.

6a. Fold the triangle at the pointed end back and forth, making sharp creases. Leave triangle in previous position.

6b. Fold the front flap from left to right. Repeat on the back.

7. On the front, fold the top edge to the middle. As the paper moves down, squash the corner to form a triangle. This is tricky. Do the same with the bottom edge. Turn the paper over and repeat on the back.

8. Fold front flap from right to left. Repeat on the back.

9. Grasp both ends—one end with each hand—and pull gently apart. Poke the blunt end of a pencil around the inside of the central opening. Sharply crease the outside edges of the square.

10. Form a ring by sliding one end of the ring into the pleats at the other end.

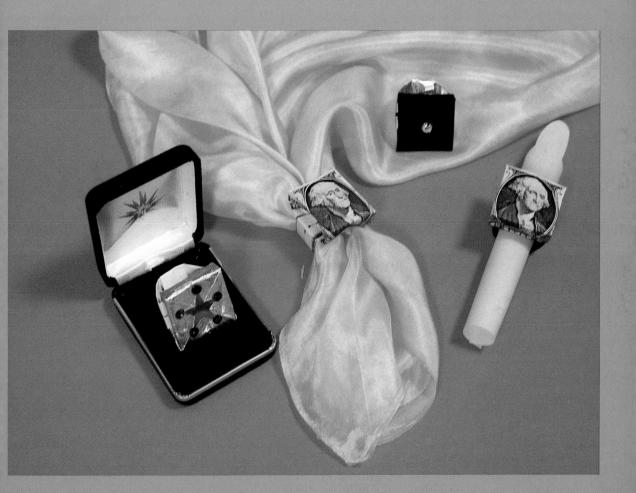

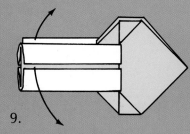

9.

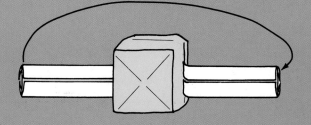

BUTTERFLIES

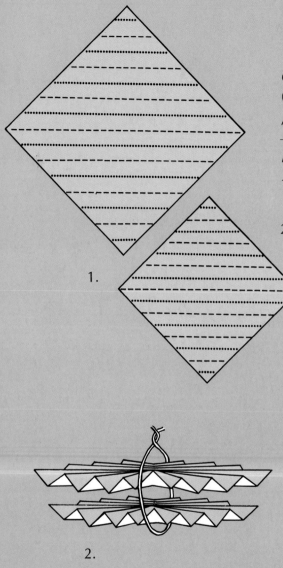

1.

2.

BUTTERFLIES

You need:

One 3 inch (8 cm) paper square and a $2\frac{1}{2}$ inch (6 cm) paper square

A wire twist

Pleat each square in the same way.

1. Fan pleat back and forth on the diagonal. Paper will have eight ribs.

2. Tie the pleated papers together with a wire twist. Curl the wire ends, snipping off any extra. Spread the wings.

HAIR ORNAMENT, WRISTLET OR PIN

Glue a folded butterfly:

To a hair barrette or comb (for a hair ornament); to a yard ($\frac{1}{2}$ m) of ribbon (for a wristlet); or to a $1\frac{1}{2}$ inch (4 cm) pin back (for a pin).

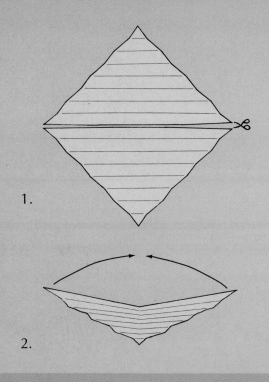

1.

2.

EARRINGS

You need:

One $3\frac{1}{2}$ inch (9 cm) paper square

Earring fittings

---

1. Pleat the square in the same way as for the butterfly. Cut the paper on the middle crease.

2. Fold each piece of pleated paper in half (see next drawing).

3. Spread the pleats. If desired, glue the two straight edges together.

4. Attach earring fittings.

HELPFUL HINTS

KEY

Crease paper up

Crease paper backward (away from you)

Thin line—existing crease made before

Arrow points in the direction in which paper is to be folded

Make a crease and unfold it

Turn paper over

··
Valley Fold

— — — — — — — — — —
Mountain Fold

_____
Existing Crease

Direction to fold

Fold/Unfold

Back to front

PAPERS

Origami squares are colored on the front and white on the back. Some origami squares are patterned or colored differently on the front and the back.Try these other lightweight papers which crease well and can be cut to size: giftwrap, foil giftwrap (not kitchen foil), stationery, water color, handmade, computer papers and magazine pages. You can make two-color paper by gluing together the backs of two pieces of paper; glue papers first, then cut to size.

GLUES

White glue is recommended. To prevent wrinkling, use only the smallest amount necessary. Duco cement is suggested for attaching earring and other fittings.

FINISH

Brush jewelry with two thin coats of white glue, if desired. It will dry transparent and stiff. Always rinse brush immediately after each use. Jewelry made from foil giftwrap does not need to be coated.

ATTACHING EARRINGS

Instant Fittings
Knot loops of thread through the top of earrings. Or use rubber bands which have been cut open. Either way hang the loops around the ears.

Fittings from Craft and Bead Stores
For pierced ears: Pierce a hole with a pin at the top of the earring and insert a wire loop
                         fitting.
For non-pierced ears: Glue clips to the back of the earrings. For dangling earrings, use special
                         earring clips with rings to hang wire loop fittings.